FUCK ALCOHOL

Addiction Rehab
COLORING BOOK

In the same collection

FUCK ADDICTION

Sobriety

Coloring Journal

Scan to watch on amazon.com

IT DOESN'T MATTER
how slowly
YOU GO
AS LONG AS YOU
don't
STOP

NOT
easy
BUT
worth
IT

recovery
IS
ABOUT
Progression
NOT
Perfection

FUCK
ALCOHOL

SOBER
forever

BELIEVE
IN
yourself

DO NOT
give
UP

ONE
day
AT A
TIME

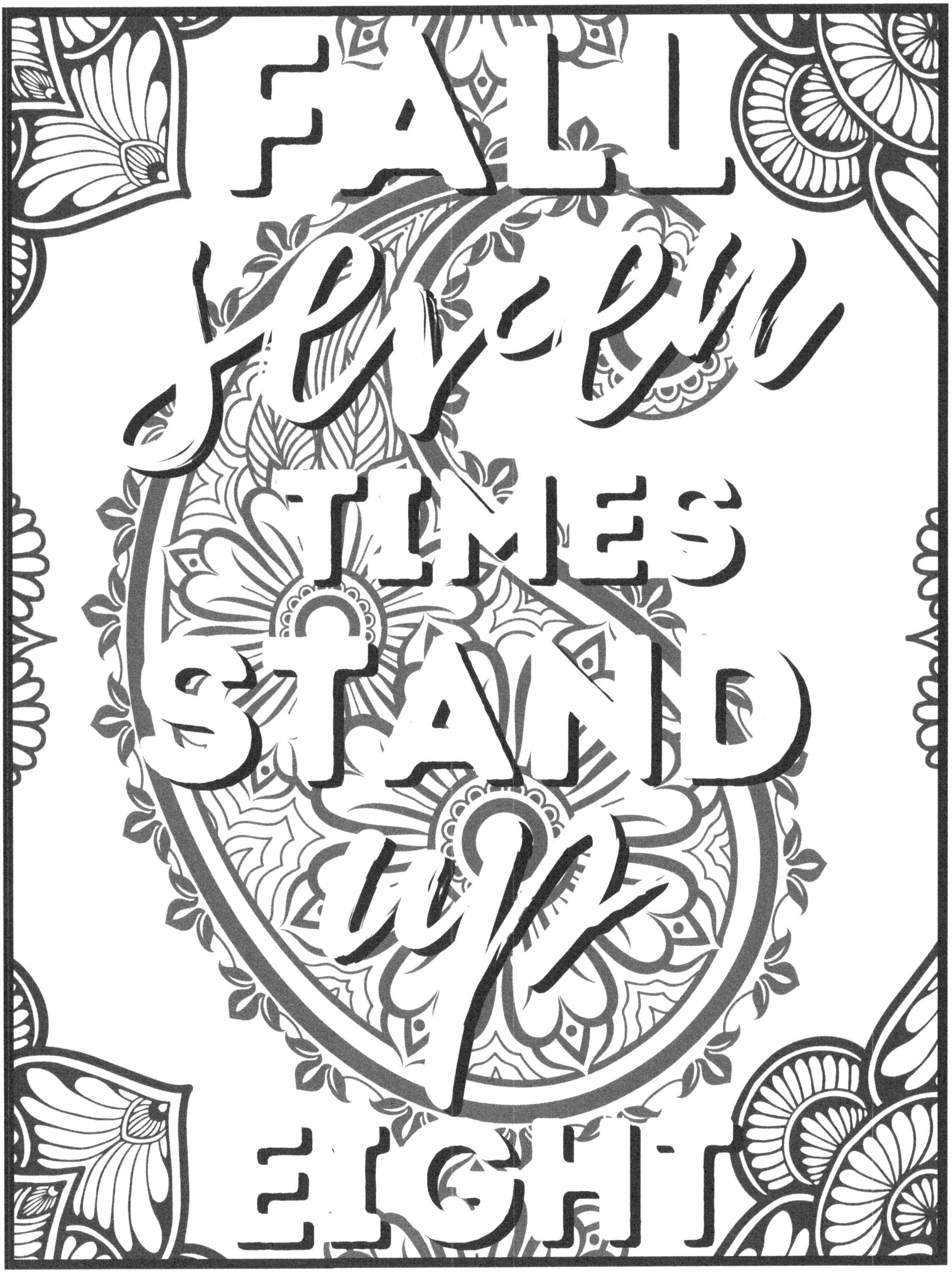
FALL
seven
TIMES
STAND
up
EIGHT

LOVE
yourself
SO MUCH
THAT
you don't
NEED TO
drink

TODAY
is gonna
BE A
FUCKING
Good
DAY

I AM
Fucking
AWESOME

Sending
HELP

Fuck
EXCUSES

Wake
UP
Fuck
ALCOHOL
and
REPEAT

Sober
AND
STRONG

Sober
AS
FUCK

STOP
drinking
GET
Shit
DONE

LIVING
Sober
IS A
GIFT
from
GOD

DRINKING
Kills
COLORING
Heals

DRINK
Water
SURPRISE
YOUR
Liver

STOP
drinking
START
living

I
REFUSE
TO
Sink

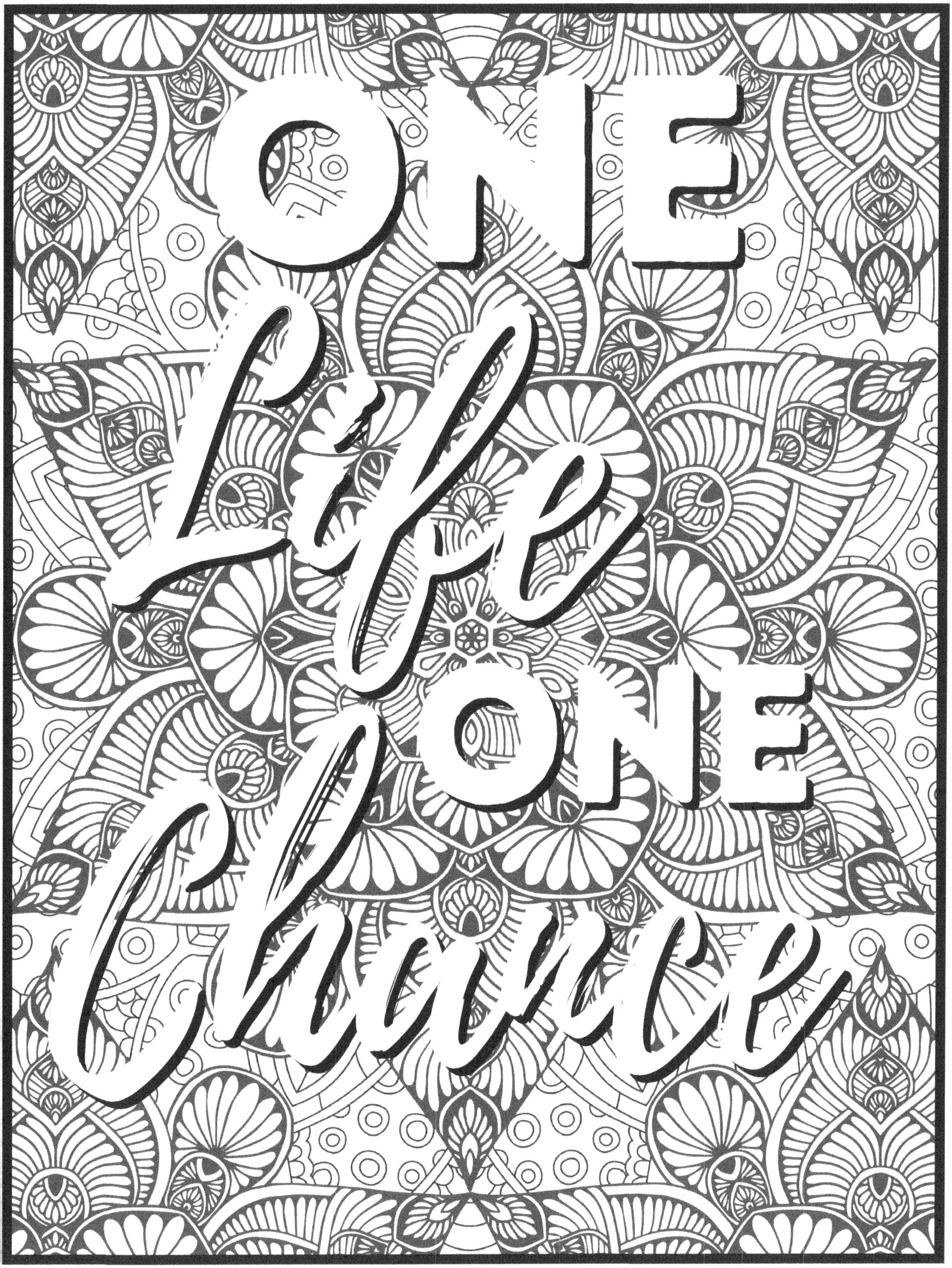
ONE
Life
ONE
Chance

MY
Story
ISN'T
OVER
yet

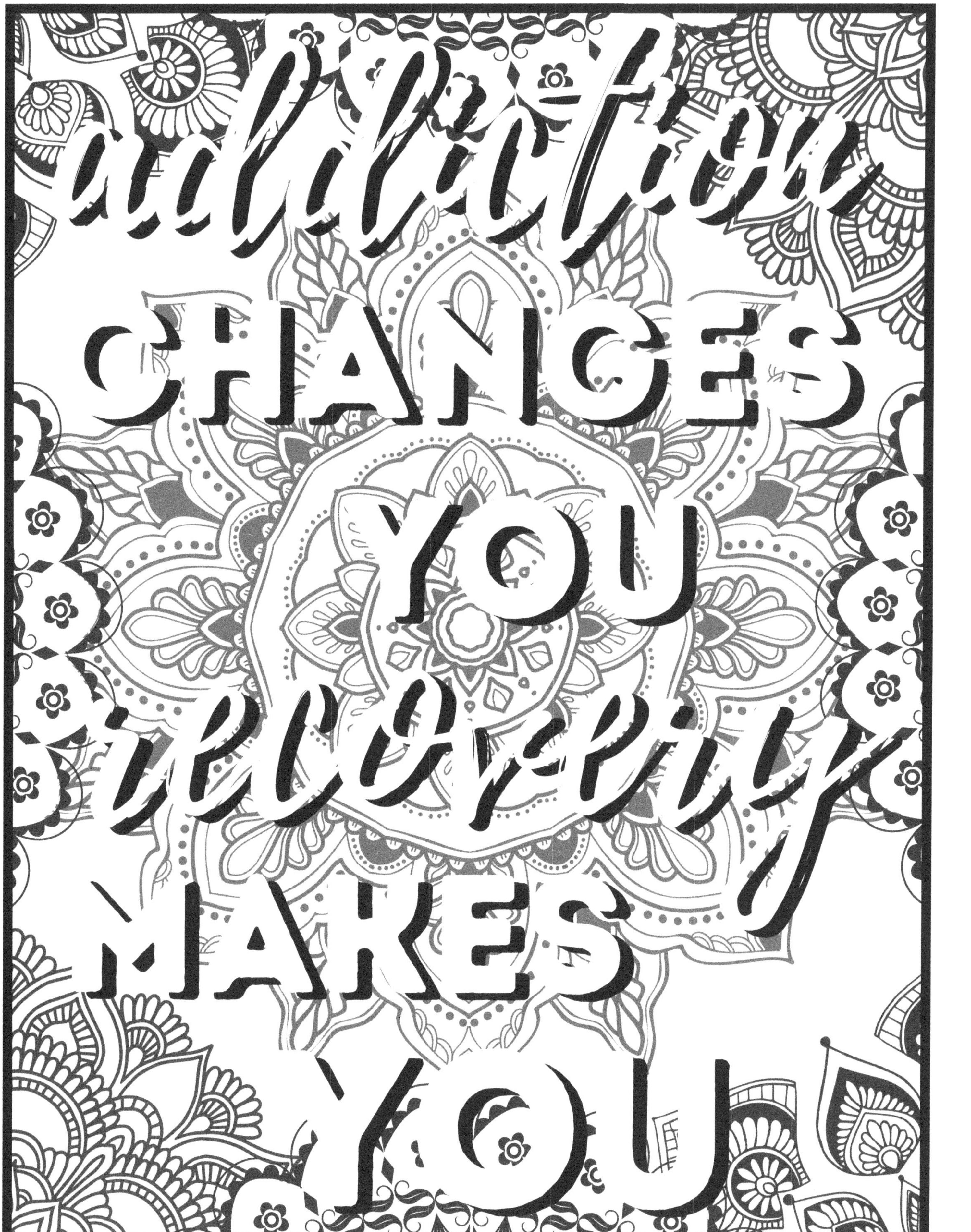
addiction
CHANGES
YOU
recovery
MAKES
YOU

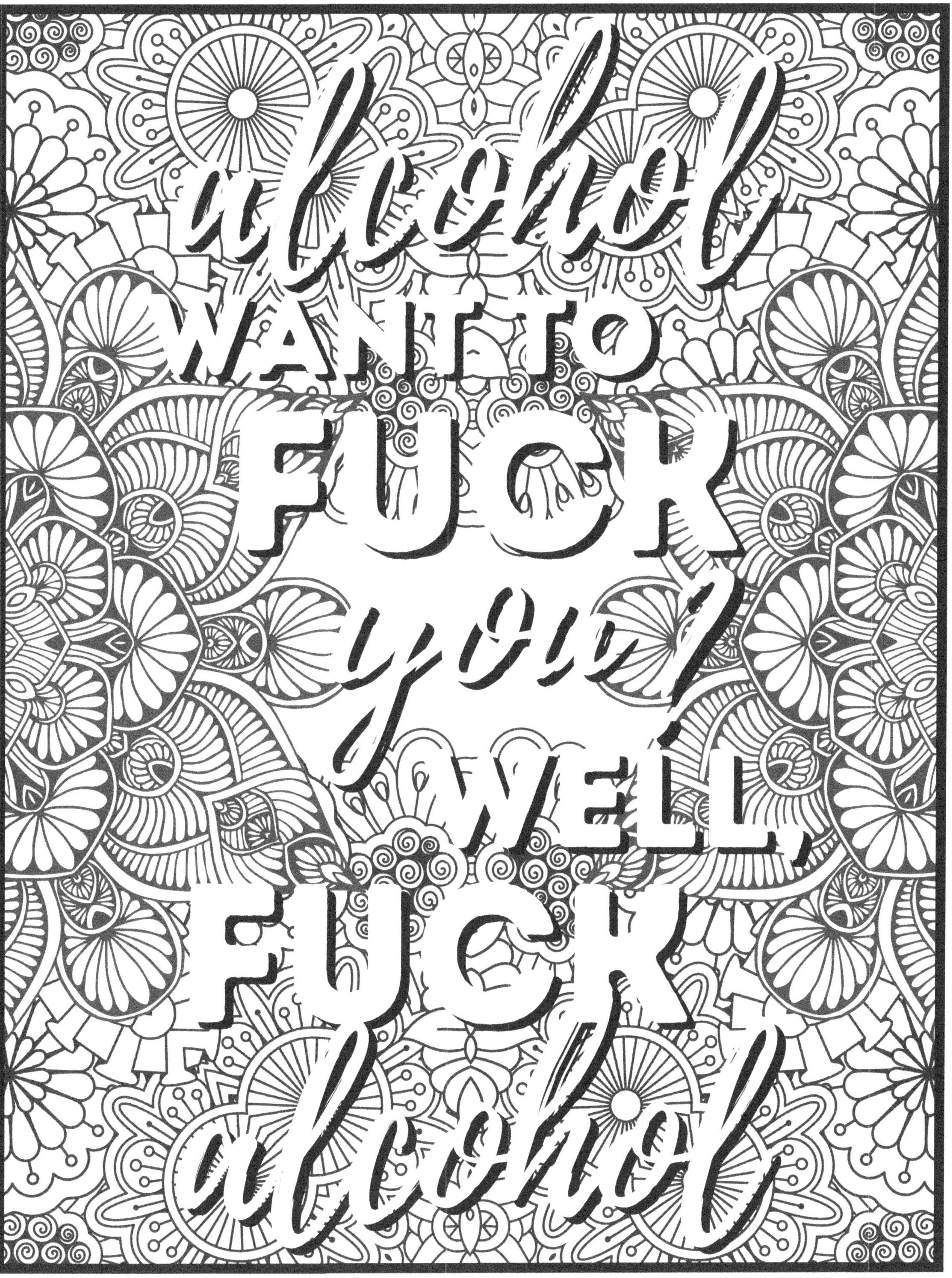
alcohol
WANT TO
FUCK
you?
WELL,
FUCK
alcohol

Made in the USA
Las Vegas, NV
03 February 2024

85257931R00033